About the Author:

Glenn Davison designs, builds, and flies kites using a wide variety of reclaimed, recycled, and free materials.

He has written several books, "Kites in the Classroom," "How to Fly a Kite," "Miniature Kites," "Indoor Kite Flying," and the "Kite Workshop Handbook."

He has been the president of a kite club, Director of the American Kitefliers Association, Chairman of the Kite Education Committee, and he has led dozens of kite workshops.

Overview:

This book describes many ways to build kites for free using recycled, organic, or found materials so the kite costs little or nothing to build and fly!

(c) 2017 Glenn Davison, all rights reserved.

Bell Tetra kite made from dowels and colored spotlight gels.

Contents

History

Kites have a long history that goes back thousands of years. Kites have been made from everything you can imagine. Bamboo and paper continue to be widely used for making kites worldwide. From the fighter kites of India to the giant kites in Japan to the animal kites in China, all kinds of kites have been built using a variety of bamboo and paper.

But what about candy wrappers? Could they fly? What about bags and wrapping paper? Or tissue paper?

If you were working alone you could try many variations of spar length, spar placement, spar flexibility, bridle lines, angle of attack, kite height, and kite wingspan. You could continue to experiment to find the sweet spot but this book has information and plans make the process easy.

A flapping bird kite made from a plastic bag and bamboo.

Bet you didn't know...

...that people flew kites 1,000 years before paper was invented! The first kites were flown over 3000 years ago and were actually made of leaves. In Indonesia leaf kites are still used for fishing today!

Kites have a long history of reuse

For more than a hundred years, kites have been built out of basic household items and whatever materials were nearby. They weren't ideal materials but they were freely available.

Bedsheets were torn into strips and spars were carved from fallen branches or wooden slats. Butcher paper and newspaper were used along with paste and rough twine. Certainly those kites needed more wind to compensate for the extra weight. The materials and the plans used were not optimized for flying.

Some of those traditions are still alive today and some of the kites built that way fly beautifully. Paper and bamboo are an example of traditional materials that have been used to build a wide variety of ornate kites.

Today we are surrounded by more thin, light materials than ever before. Manufacturers are constantly trying to save money by using thinner plastic. Some plastic sheets are only microns in thickness. Paper and plastic are consistent and so abundant that they are frequently discarded.

Everything we need is nearby and just like in yesteryears it's free.

Bet you didn't know...

...that the first delta kite was built by Francis and Gertrude Rogallo, when they constructed the prototype by reusing their kitchen curtains!

Building kites is rewarding for all ages

Building a kite can provide a quick result even if you have never built a kite before. You'll smile when you see your kite in the sky. It's worth it! There is always the fascination of flight.

Everyone enjoys the hands-on experience of building and flying their own work of art. When you build a kite there's a pride of ownership that is stronger than when you buy a kite.

Start today. Gather the necessary materials over time and check your recycle bin, it may be filled with treasures!

Building a recycled kite will:

- Give a sense of accomplishment.
- Encourage building instead of buying.
- Provide real-world applications of science, math, and art skills.
- Provide an opportunity for teamwork.
- Encourage you to find and compare alternate solutions to a problem.
- Give kite builders an opportunity to practice skills like measurement, following directions, and solving problems.

Tip: For suggestions on purchasing materials, see the supplies section at the end of this book.

Materials

It's amazing what you can find when you look for lightweight materials to build a kite. Check around the house and in your recycle bin for discarded or unused items. Simply asking for donations is a great way to get materials for free.

The materials you use depend on the kite you're building. For large kites you will need to pair a combination of strong sails and spars to handle the force of the wind without breaking. Small kites need to be lightweight in order to fly at all.

Paper kites can be simple while large, sewn kites can become very complex and may require specialized materials like fittings, ferrules, standoffs, nocks, and end caps.

The four most important parts are:

- **Sail** – these can be nylon, paper, or plastic.
- **Tail** – these can be nylon, paper, or plastic.
- **Flying line** – also called, "string" of cotton, polyester, etc.
- **Spars** – the spine is vertical, the spreader is horizontal.

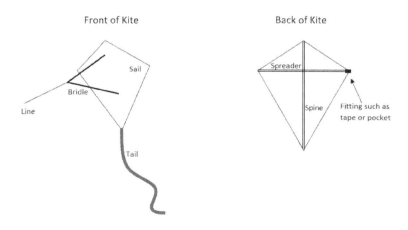

9

Materials typically found at home

Look around your home. You might already have some of these materials:

- Bamboo meat skewers
- Bamboo lawn stakes
- Straws
- Garbage bags
- Plastic shopping bags
- Copy paper
- Tissue paper
- Shipping tape
- Cellophane tape
- Thread
- Twine
- Dental floss

Note: Some towns have banned plastic bags from the recycling process. Your town may not allow you to put plastic bags in your recycle bin but reusing them is an ideal alternative.

Kite bag made by recycling the sail from a windsurfer.

Sail Materials

The most popular sail materials include plastic garbage bags, Dry Cleaner bags, tissue paper, wrapping paper, typing paper, ripstop nylon, and Tyvek®. Paper and plastic are the least expensive while ripstop nylon and Tyvek® are more durable. All of them make great kite sails.

Dry Cleaner bags – these are free, large, and very thin. They can be decorated with markers and reinforced with colorful tape.

Garbage bags – can be purchased at all supermarkets. You can easily make comparisons because the thickness of the plastic is printed on every box in micrometers. Avoid the pleated plastic bags that are designed to stretch or flex.

Nylon scraps - Legend has it that people have recycled nylon parachute fabric, hot air balloon fabric, and boat sails. One of these might provide a lifetime supply of fabric for you and your friends! Although these are heavy, they are great for making kite bags.

Nylon umbrellas – are often discarded when the mechanism becomes bent or broken. The fabric is usually intact and the nylon is perfect for building large kites.

Picnic table cover – these are large vinyl or plastic sheets that are lightweight. They are 40 sq. ft. (7 sq. meters).

Plastic shopping bags – They are free and plentiful from Supermarkets and drug stores. These thin plastic bags are provided for free at checkout and are ideal for kites. Collect a few of these bags and keep an eye out for different colors. Many are printed with store logos.

Plastic Trash bags - A great place to start is with tall plastic kitchen bags. Each box is labeled with the thickness of the plastic in micrometers and the thinnest bags are often the least expensive. Buy a box and experiment!

Tip: Do not use bags that stretch because they are more difficult to work with and may result in a loose or uneven kite sail.

Produce bags – similar to plastic shopping bags, these clear plastic bags are provided by supermarkets. They are provided on a roll so shoppers can take a bag and fill it with fruits or vegetables. They're thin, free, and very lightweight.

Shower curtains and liners – these plastic or nylon sheets are large, heavy, and strong. They can be cleaned in the washing machine by combining baking soda, laundry detergent, and towels. Rinse them with vinegar.

This Pipa combat kite was made with tissue paper by Vinnie.

Telephone book pages - The pages of a telephone book provide hundreds of thin sheets of paper in white and yellow.

Tissue paper - Lightweight with a wide assortment of colors and patterns.

Tyvek envelopes – available for free at the post office. These are very tough and will not tear. Tyvek is used as a house wrap during construction. It is widely available in large white rolls.

Tyvek® rolls - Tyvek can be used in the same ways you use paper but it is much stronger. You can get Tyvek Post Office envelopes for free. Tyvek is used in house construction as a vapor barrier, and a soft variety is made into suits for handling hazardous materials. Avoid pre-printed Tyvek because the lettering shows though when your kite is in the sky.

Wrapping tissue and tissue paper – some stores wrap products with tissue to protect them. Such items include glass, china, shoes, and jewelry. Wrapping tissue and tissue paper can also be purchased at dollar stores in a variety of colors, patterns, themes, and characters.

Line, string materials

Flying line needs to be long, strong, thin, and lightweight. The flying line should be matched to the size of the kite and the current wind speed.

Often the most expensive part of a recycled kite is the line. If you're ready to spend money for good line, it can be purchased on handles, spools, or in bulk.

Line made from cotton, nylon, and Dacron polyester is available in a wide variety of lengths and strengths.

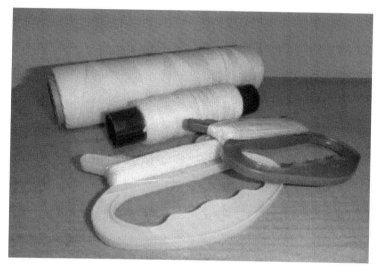

It may be difficult to find the right kite line for free. However, there are alternatives, including:

Baker's twine – cotton string sold in rolls for cooking.

Button thread – is a thick, heavy duty thread you may find at garage sales and sewing stores.

Dental floss – easy to find and strong but more expensive than kite string.

Fishing line – ask a fisherman for his unused or old line.

Kite line – find a kite store or ask a kite flier if they have extra or wish to buy in bulk and share the cost.

Measuring line or Builder's line – available at hardware stores.

Twine – available at hardware stores.

Yarn – available at crafts stores but it is bulky.

Tip: Braided kite line is superior to twisted line because it's less prone to twisting and knotting.

Tip: Don't use monofilament fishing line because it is too elastic and may burn your fingers. Braided line is preferred.

Tip: Don't use any line that's so heavy that it will sag while the kite is flying. If it does, switch to a thinner, lighter line.

Tip: To be prepared for light wind and heavy wind conditions, always carry lines that vary in strength.

Line holders

Once you have kite line you may want a convenient way to store it, carry it with you, and retrieve it once the flying is done.

<u>Tip</u>: Don't wind your line around a wooden craft stick because the diameter is so small that it doesn't store much line and it takes too long to wind it up!

There are many alternatives. You can wrap 30' to 50' (10 to 15 meters) of heavy duty thread around a:

- Plastic credit card or gift card (Best)
- Plastic water bottle
- Piece of cardboard from any box
- Toilet paper cardboard tube
- Roll of junk mail
- Stick of wood

<u>Tip</u>: Use scissors to make a small cut that will hold the end of the thread securely and prevent it from unraveling.

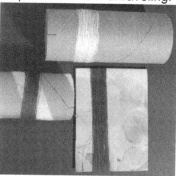

<u>Tip</u>: Wrap the line holder with heavy duty tape to make it more durable and colorful.

Bamboo mats - These are available as placemats or Sushi and Maki rolling mats. By cutting the supporting strings you get hundreds of bamboo strips.

Bamboo poles - Bamboo poles and bamboo plant stakes are packaged and sold in the gardening section of home improvement stores. They can be split into strips or used whole.

Bamboo skewers - Bamboo skewers are used for grilling meat and vegetables. They are widely available in supermarkets and can be used directly without the need to split them.

Tip: You should remove the sharp point from the end of the skewer using a clipper, heavy-duty scissors, or a rotary tool.

Coffee stirrers - Coffee shops and fast food restaurants provide free plastic and wood stirrers. The length and diameter varies.

Dowels – solid wooden dowels can be purchased at craft stores.

Fiberglass rods - Many hardware stores carry these rods to mark the location of a garden or driveway. These rods are solid and very strong but they are also heavy compared to other alternatives. Use them for kites that are 5' or larger.

Caution: Some types of fiberglass have sharp slivers along their length. Use gloves to protect your hands.

Marshmallow sticks - These birch dowels are long and light. You can find these in some supermarkets.

Straws – Many fast food shops provide free plastic straws. Avoid the straws that have a bend in them because they will allow your kite to flex in the wrong location.

Window shades, blinds, bamboo panels – are made of horizontal strips of bamboo that are sometimes called, "matchstick bamboo" because of the small diameter of the sticks. These are held tightly together by strings. Simply cut the strings to release hundreds of long pieces of bamboo. You may be able to find them at import stores or discount shops. Sometimes you can find a window blind that's broken and get it at a discount.

Tail Materials

Tails can be made from a variety of materials:

Cloth cut from bed sheets can be tied together to create long, strong tails. They may be too heavy for some kites.

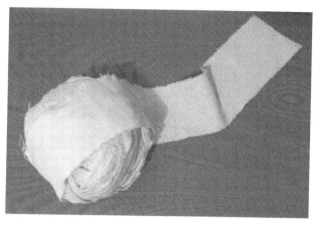

Crepe paper is widely available at party stores. It is lightweight and inexpensive but it tears too easily.

Fuzzy tails - can be created easily by reinforcing the center then cutting into the tail with a razor knife.

Photo by Bob and Charmayne Umbowers.

Marking tape is a favorite tail material that is used by many kite builders. Also called "flagging tape" it is sold in most hardware stores. Even though it's called "tape" it's really a streamer without adhesive so it's perfect for kite tails.

Plastic bags can easily be cut into strips for tails. The strips can be used individually or taped together to make long streamers.

Ribbons are available in a wide variety of colors. They're great if you have them at home, but they are can be expensive to buy when compared to other alternatives.

VCR tapes and cassette tapes are thin and lightweight. Just a single cassette can provide enough tails for hundreds of small kites. These are highly conductive so keep them away from power lines.

Organic materials

Bamboo

In some areas of the world bamboo grows naturally and can be cut, dried, and split into strong, lightweight and flexible strips. The thickness of the strip determines its flexibility. To find good bamboo see: http://www.guaduabamboo.com/working-with-bamboo/splitting-bamboo

Leaves

Certain large leaves have been used for kites for years and may have been the basis of the first kites ever flown.

Palm fronds

For long, light spars, dry the broad palm leaves then strip them of leaves. Do not remove them from the trees, find ones that are already down.

Reeds

Reeds are abundant including reed sweetgrass, reed canary-grass, and others.

Cattail (also called, "bulrush")

This plant is found in North, South America, Europe, Eurasia, and Africa.

The long stalks are stiff and lightweight. After you cut and dry them you may need to split them. If you do experiment with them, share your experiences online or use the contact information on the final page.

Holding it all together

They say that duct tape is what holds the world together. That's rarely true for kites. There are plenty of lightweight alternatives to duct tape including:

- Cellophane tape (lightest tape)
- Plastic shipping tape
- Strapping tape
- Glue, super-glue, cement, and adhesives
- Soldering iron – for melting plastic together

Plastic shipping tape:

Cellophane tape is available in many colors and patterns:

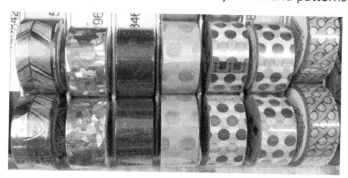

Weight comparisons

These numbers should give you a general idea of the weights of different materials. Keep in mind that the weight of spars and sails vary by thickness.

Spars: (sample size 8" or 20 cm)

Matchstick bamboo (1/10")	0.5 grams
Coffee stirrer made of plastic	0.6 grams
Plastic straw	0.7 grams
Paper straw	0.8 grams
Bamboo meat skewer (12" or 30 cm)	0.9 grams
Coffee stirrer made of wood	1.0 grams
Dowel (1/8" or 3 mm)	1.1 grams
Bamboo meat skewer (30" or 76 cm)	3.5 grams

Sails: (sample size 8.5" x 11" or 22 cm x 28 cm)

Plastic produce bag	0.4 grams
Dry Cleaner bag	0.5 grams
Tissue paper	1.1 grams
Plastic garbage bag	1.4 grams
Nylon fabric	2.9 grams
Wrapping paper	3.4 grams
Tyvek	4.0 grams
Typing paper	4.5 grams

Adhesives: (sample size 12" or 30 cm)

Cellophane tape	0.3 grams
Shipping tape	0.7 grams
Duct tape	3.7 grams

<u>Note</u>: For ounces, divide the number of grams by 28.35

Materials to avoid

When choosing materials, it's important to know what to avoid. In general, avoid anything that's too heavy for the size of kite that you want to build or too stiff or delicate causing the kite to break or tear. Also avoid spars that are so flexible that they offer no resistance to the wind. Avoid materials such as:

Cardboard and cardboard tubes – these are too easily cracked, creased and broken.

Chopsticks – are too heavy, too stiff, and difficult to split.

Cloth – Avoid cotton cloth, silk cloth, or any fabric that stretches. There are many lightweight alternatives.

Duct Tape – great stuff, but there are lighter alternatives.

Long spars – If you're building a big kite, make sure it can break down for storage using ferrule tubes or hinges.

Metal – it's just too heavy. There are many better alternatives.

Newspaper – too easily torn. Trash bags are lighter and stronger. If you have your heart set on newsprint, use a page of comics for colorful results.

Plastic wrap – too stretchy.

Stretch bags - avoid puckered trash bags designed to stretch.

Straws that bend – most plastic straws have a bend in them while a kite needs them to be strong and straight. Avoid them.

Toilet paper – is difficult to decorate and rips too easily.

Wax paper – the surface is difficult to glue, tape, and decorate.

Wild ideas - materials to try

Here are some wild ideas to help you build some unusual kites:

- Disposable Tyvek White Coverall Suit kite

- Supermarket poster kite

- Shower curtain kite

- Foam floor insulation kite – this is available in rolls at building supply stores.

- Rain poncho kite – made of vinyl. These are available in children's and adult's sizes

- Cardboard box cellular kite – just remove the kittens and tinker with a 3-point bridle.

- Bubble wrap kite – Yes, it's been done!

- Plastic Drop Cloth - that protects furniture from paint, the size is a huge 9 feet x 12 feet (2.74m x 3.65m)

Quad-line kite made from a garbage bag by Art St. Pierre

Combining materials to form a balanced kite

A kite can be described as an object that creates a balance in flight. If you want to build a symmetric kite, make sure the left side is identical to the right. Your kite should also be balanced in size, weight, and flexibility with the left side again equal to the right. Most importantly the kite should be lightweight for its size.

Starting small and progressing to large kites, here are some combinations that work well together:

Sail +	Spars +	Line
Tissue paper	Straws	Thread
Tissue paper	Strips of bamboo	Thread
Plastic shopping bag	Bamboo skewers	Dental floss
Plastic garbage bag	1/8"(3 mm) dowels	Dental floss
Nylon or polyester ripstop fabric	Fiberglass rods	50# or higher Dacron line
Nylon or polyester ripstop fabric	Carbon fiber tubes	50# or higher Dacron line

Tip: Use tissue paper for your small kites, say less than 3 feet (1 meter). Use nylon and polyester for your largest kites, say larger than 3 feet (1 meter). Plastic can be used for all kite sizes depending on the thickness.

Tools

The tools you'll need vary by project. Even if the materials are free, having the proper tools will make your project go faster and easier.

For paper and plastic kites

Some typical tools that are used for kite making paper kites include: scissors, craft knife, ruler, tape, glue, pens, pencils, markers, and possibly a paper cutter or paper punch.

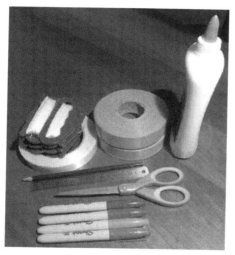

For sewn kites

Some typical tools that are used for sewn kites may include: a sewing machine, extension cord, power strip, light, spare bobbins, thread, needles, a needle threading tool, seam tape, seam ripper, pencil, ruler, scissors, appliqué scissors, pliers, hot knife, hot tacker, or soldering iron.

Techniques

Tails

How to make tails from recycled plastic bags

For a quick and easy way to make tails:

1. Take a plastic sheet or bag and lay it flat.

2. If you're using a plastic bag, start with the closed end and roll the bag into a long tight tube:

3. Use scissors to cut the tube into many small chunks. They are 2" (5 cm) wide but still tightly rolled:

4. Unroll your chunks and use tape to attach them together to make long tails for your kite!

Spars

Making long sticks from short ones

Cut the two spars at an angle before you rejoin them with glue. This will increase the surface area of two spars forming a stronger bond:

Overlapping and gluing spars works well too. Wrapping them with thread adds strength:

Two sticks can be joined using a ferrule tube cut from the shell of a ball point pen:

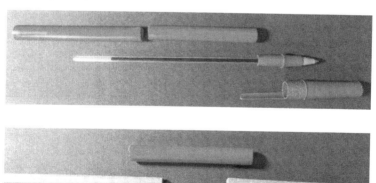

Splitting bamboo

Dry your bamboo then split it using a sharp knife. Start the split, then use a twisting motion continue the split down the length of the bamboo. Always use responsible adult supervision when handling sharp knives.

As an alternative, you can use bamboo window shades. They are a great source of bamboo and no splitting is necessary.

Curving a bamboo spreader

Test the curve of a piece of bamboo by flexing it. The result should be an even curve. If the curve is uneven, sand or shave the flat side of the bamboo to create an even curve.

 Too thick

Strengthening wood

Diagonally wrap the wood with a covering of paper and glue to add strength. Wrapping tape over the wood joint works too. Both techniques add weight that may not be necessary.

Bending bamboo

To bend bamboo you can heat it with a candle or hot halogen light. It becomes soft and flexible then hardens when it cools.

Joining straws

You can join straws but even though this technique is weak, you might find it useful. Tuck the end of one straw inside the next then use cellophane tape to hold them together.

Making a spar-to-spar connection

To join spars, glue two small dowels to your spar. It acts like a fork making it easy to connect to another spar at a right angle.

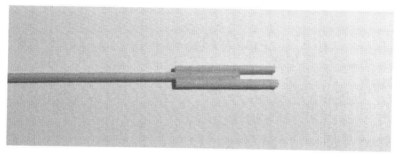

Creating pockets for spars

The simplest way to attach a spar to a sail is to tape it in place by folding the tape over the edge of the sail:

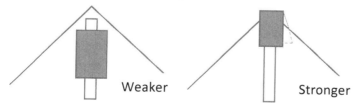

Weaker   Stronger

Cellophane tape is fine for small paper and plastic kites. If you need more strength, use strapping tape. It has fibers embedded in the tape that make it far stronger.

Creating a center connector for spars

- I thought I invented this method of connecting spars but I've seen it elsewhere called a "pig nose." To create a free connector for two spars, cut a plastic rectangle then fold it around the spine. Use a hole-punch or a drill to create holes on either side. Wrap it around the spine and pass the spreader through it. Tape the spine in place to prevent the connector from shifting up or down.

- Spars can be joined using a thick rubber band or string soaked in glue.

- Another alternative is to use a "tie wrap" from a bag of bread and wrap it across the joint in an 'X' fashion.

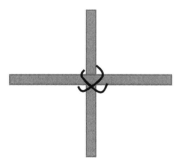

Sails

Creating symmetry for a sail

Here's a simple technique to ensure that the left and right sides of your kite are identical: Fold the paper or plastic in half and cut both sides at the same time.

Joining sheets of paper

- Use a glue stick for a quick paper bond.
- To spread glue evenly on paper, put white or yellow glue on one of the pieces of paper then spread it evenly using an old credit card. This will avoid lumps and missed spots.
- Use spray adhesive.
- Use double-sided tape.
- Make your own glue using water and flour by searching the web for "recipes-to-make-your-own-glue"

Separating napkins

Paper napkins have thousands of interesting designs. With care, you can carefully separate the layers of a napkin by peeling the 2-ply layers of the napkin apart. This results in a thin, lightweight paper sail that's great for a small kite.

Joining sheets of plastic

Often you'll find plastic bags aren't large enough for a project. You can join them with an iron on the polyester setting or you can use double-sided tape. Both methods allows you to attach sheets together to create a patchwork style. Joining sheets with a strip of tape also adds strength.

To join sheets with tape:

Use masking tape to hold the first sheet down to the table so it's smooth. Alternatively, spraying a thin mist of water onto the table will hold the plastic in place while you tape.

1. Use double-sided cellophane tape near one edge
2. Overlap the second sheet
3. Press firmly along the tape
4. Carefully cut the excess from both sides

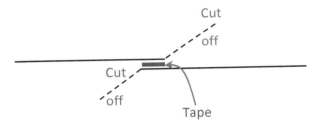

A sled kite made from plastic bags
taped together with double-sided tape.

Using templates

Templates are important because they provide an easy method for tracing the outline onto the sail material. Templates make it easy to build a kite accurately and repeatedly.

Tip: Many templates are provided as a "half template." These require that the sail be folded in half, then draw the outline onto the sail, then cut along the outline. By using a half template, even if a mistake is made while cutting, both halves of the sail are still symmetrical. This is important for steady flight.

Tip: Cut up a pizza box to make a free template.

Tip: Thick paper works and you can always tape smaller pieces together to make a larger template.

Templates usually indicate critical details such as: the bridle points, the locations of the spars, the locations of the tape, the top, the front, and any special instructions.

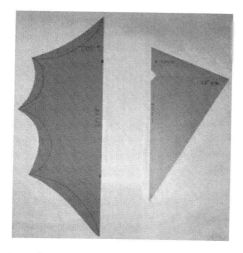

Two examples of templates, each indicate the bridle points.

Creating beauty through decoration

Adding decorations to your kite will turn a plain white kite into a masterpiece! Even the simplest kite can become a beautiful work of art. When people decorate their kites it becomes a personal statement, something valuable and something worth keeping.

Tip: Markers are recommended for decorating kites because they result in bright colors with very little weight. Markers are available in many colors and don't require any cleanup.

Markers have disadvantages too. Permanent markers are not washable, they can stain clothes, they can bleed through thin paper, and they can leave marks on tables that are difficult to remove. Hence, you should protect the tables with rolls of butcher paper or plastic trash bags. Consider washable markers for decorating paper kites.

Building and decorating a kite gives immediate satisfaction.

<u>Tip</u>: When decorating a kite, avoid decorations that involve extra weight such as glitter glue, stickers, or tape.

With that in mind, here's a kite that breaks the rules. It's a kite by Art St. Pierre that uses tape to create a vibrant image:

The bridle

The bridle adjusts the angle of flight and can significantly improve the flight of your kite. It is the most important feature of your new kite and must be done correctly for the kite to fly.

1. **Set the bridle**
   Lay the prototype kite on the ground then lift up by pulling slowly on the bridle. The top of the kite should lift off the ground before the rest of the kite rises.

2. **Balance the weight of the kite**
   One side of a kite (the left side) may be lighter or heavier than the other (the right side). To check this, dangle the kite from the bridle. The kite should hang flat. If it does not, add small bits of tape to the tip of the side that is lighter, or the side that is higher than the other. Add tape until the kite hangs flat.

3. **Test the bridle in the wind**
   The small attachment point below shows a possible location where the string should be attached to the bridle. It's called the "tow point" and it is critical. Move the tow point up or down in quarter inch (1/2 cm) increments until the kite flies steadily. Small changes can make a big difference. To find the best tow point, pinch the bridle with two fingers, hold the kite in the wind, then slide the bridle up or down in ¼" (5 mm) increments until the kite flies smoothly.

<u>Tip</u>: A good starting point is to use a two-point bridle then make adjustments outdoors.

Example: two-point bridle:

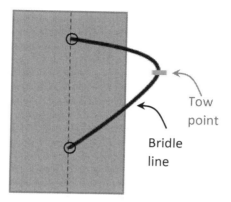

Tow point

Bridle line

Notice that the top part of the loop above is shorter than the bottom of the loop. This correctly tilts the top of the kite into the wind.

Example: three-point bridle:

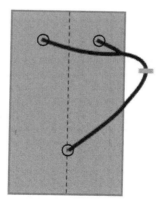

Adding Tails

Some kites don't require tails but when your kite sways left and right, add more tails, even if it has a tail already. Tails also add beauty and drama.

Tails can be clipped on or attached with a slip knot. This makes it easy to switch the tails from one kite to another.

Tip: Start with one tail that's seven times the height of your kite.

Tip: Always adjust the bridle first to get the best angle of attack, then add additional tails as needed.

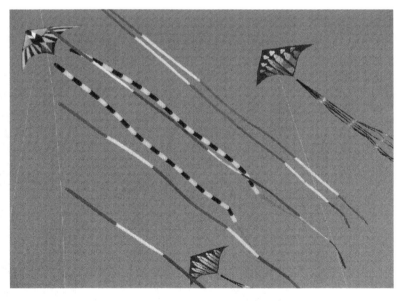

Tails add beauty, color, and drama.

Flying your kite

To choose a flying location, launch, fly, and retrieve a kite, see the book, "How to Fly a Kite" available from the American Kitefliers Association.

Tip: Find a flying location that is far from trees and buildings and has clear access to the wind.

You do not need to run to launch a kite and never run in circles or throw the kite into the air.

Tip: Pay attention to the wind direction and remember to keep your back to the wind.

The goal in launching a kite is to get the kite into the steady stream of wind above the trees and buildings. The best way to do this is to use a trick that kite fliers call a "long launch." One person holds the kite while the other person holds the spool. Then you dispense 50' to 100' (30 m) of string before you launch the kite. This "long launch" allows the person with the spool to pull the kite high into the air without running.

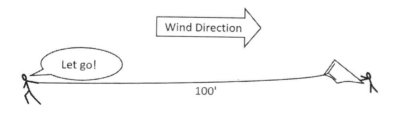

Don't limit yourself. Kites can be flown by people of all ages, throughout the year, in a variety of winds. Kites can be flown on the coldest winter days, even while it's snowing!

Flight safety

Always build and fly kites in a safe manner with responsible adult supervision.

Safety information:

- Keep far away from electrical lines and telephone poles.
- Never fly during an electrical storm.
- Fly far away from cars and roadways.
- Never fly near an airport.
- Keep away from trees and buildings.

This kite is too close to the trees and upside down!

Kite rescue and repair

Just like those who are committed to the rescue and relief of homeless animals, you can be committed. Or you can be committed to the rescue and repair of broken kites.

How? When kites break they are often placed in the trash at the end of the day. Adopt one. Frequently they need only minor repairs or extra tails to fly. Other times you can combine two broken kites into one perfect kite. If all hope is lost you can save the spars, sail, or fittings to help you build another kite.

Rescued kites make great surprises for children who don't have a kite!

Tips for building recycled kites

- <u>Avoid glue</u>, it's messy and slow. Whenever possible, use tape.
- If you need stronger tape, use "<u>strapping tape</u>" because it has strong fibers inside.
- Keep in mind that your kite should be <u>symmetric</u> in size and weight. Ensure that the sail is symmetric by folding the sail in half and cutting both sides at once.
- A <u>tail</u> should be 7-12 times the length of your kite.
- If the materials are free, <u>build two kites</u>. It doesn't take much more time and you can experiment to see what works best. If one breaks you have another!
- <u>Clear</u> plastic bags are difficult to see in the sky but can create an ethereal effect and can be decorated with markers or colorful tape.
- Always <u>replace broken spars</u>. Do not try to mend them with tape.
- Keep your spars thin. Most kites use spars that are less than ¼ inch (½ cm) in diameter.
- Make sure the spars on the left are exactly <u>equal</u> to the spars on the right side of your kite.
- Compare the <u>weight</u> of each of your choices. You may be surprised to find which material is lightest.
- Build according to one of the <u>kite plans</u> below.
- <u>Test</u> your finished kite by flying it in an open area only a short distance from your hand.
- Take <u>photos</u> and share them online.

Kite Plans

A wide variety of plans are available online. You'll find them in websites and videos but their quality varies widely.

The kites you'll find below are simple and effective. These kites are easy to build, have very few parts, and since the materials are recycled they are inexpensive or free.

Each plan gives an estimate of the building time.

Select a plan that's right for your needs based on the time, the complexity, and the materials you have available.

The plans below include:

Paper kites   These allow a wide range of creativity with markers, ink, watercolors, paint, layered paper, and decorative art paper.

Plastic kites   These are strong and lightweight.

Nylon kites   These require a sewing machine but provide the most durable results.

Paper Kites

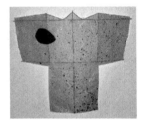

"In Belize, we used to build kites using the stalk of a coconut palm leaf to form the ribs of the kite body. We tied a string around the outside and the inside to give it strength, then covered it with crepe paper. The kites flew well on heavy duty thread."

- Reverend Earnest Belisle

Difficulty:	Easy
Time to build:	20 minutes
Size:	24" x 24" (60 cm x 60 cm)

The Eddy kite is a very popular kite style and widely recognized as a good flier.

Materials:

- SAIL: Two large sheets of newspaper or a plastic trash bag
- SPARS: Two 24" (60 cm) x 1/8" (3.2 mm) wooden dowels
- TAIL: 6' (2 m) length of marking tape, also called "Surveyor's tape or "flagging tape" or tape together 1" (2.5 cm) wide strips of plastic until they are 6' (2 m) long
- LINE: Kite string

Tools:

- Scissors
- Pencil
- Hobby knife
- Strapping tape or shipping tape
- 3" diameter bottle

Method:

1. Soak one of the 24" (60 cm) wooden dowels in water overnight. This will become your curved horizontal spreader.

2. Place the wet spreader in a drying position so that it is 3" (7.5 cm) higher at the center. This could be done on your table with a 3" (7.5 cm) bottle in the center and books to hold down the tips. Let the wooden dowel dry for 24 hours.

Book   Book

Bottle   3"

3. Fold the sail in half.

4. Match the long edge of the template to the fold in the sheet and draw the template pattern on the sail with a pencil.

5. With the sheet still folded, cut the sail along the lines from the pattern. Be sure to cut a 1" (2.5 cm) square.

6. Unfold and decorate the sail with markers. This is the front.

7. Optional: to add strength, reinforce the edge of the paper sail with cellophane tape.

8. Turn the decorated sail face down.

9. Cut eight (8) pieces of tape 3" (7 cm) in length.

10. Attach the vertical spine to the sail with tape by folding the tape over equally on front and back. The tape is on both sides and covers the end of the spar.

11. Tape the top and bottom of the spine:

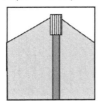 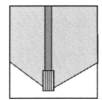

12. Attach spreader with tape on the left and right sides. The spreader should curve up and the spars should cross at the hole in the sail:

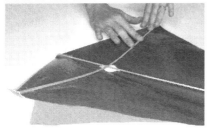

13. Align the spine and spreader then put 4 pieces of tape on them to prevent them from shifting:

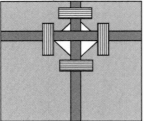

14. Attach the 6' (2 m) tail to the bottom of the spine.

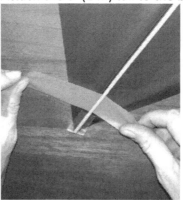

15. Turn the kite over to see the <u>front</u> of the kite. Notice that the back has the spars and the front is decorated.

16. Starting at the front, pass the string through the hole, around both spars, and back out to the front. Tie a knot. The photo shows how to start in the front and loop around both spars:

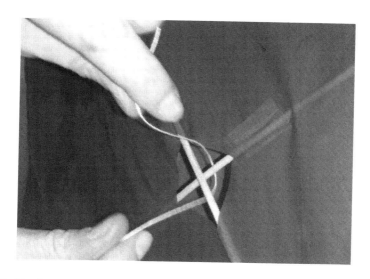

17. You're ready to fly in light or moderate wind!

<u>Quick check</u>: the spars are on the back, the flying line is on the front, and the tail is at the bottom.

Difficulty:	Easy
Time to build:	10 minutes
Size:	2" x 2.5" (5 cm x 6.5 cm)

This is a tiny kite that can be built quickly by all ages.

Materials:

- SAIL: 3" (7.5 cm) square piece of wrapping tissue (Available in flat packages, not rolls)
- SPARS: None
- TAIL: 12" (30 cm) piece of audio recording tape
- LINE: Thread

Tools:

- Pen
- Ruler
- Scissors
- Cellophane tape

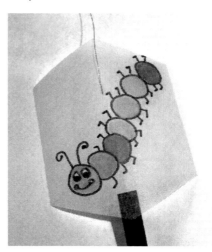

Actual size

Method:

1. Create a template 1" (2.5 cm) wide x 2.5" (6.4 cm) tall:

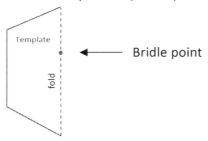

            Bridle point

2. Fold the tissue paper in half lengthwise.

3. Place the template over the folded tissue while matching the word "fold" on the template with the fold on the tissue.

4. Draw the outline of the template on the tissue paper and don't forget to mark the location of the bridle point on the tissue paper.

5. With the tissue paper folded, cut it out.

6. Unfold.

7. For a tail, cut a 12" (30 cm) strip of audio recording tape or a similar strip of tissue paper. Tape it to the back of the kite at the bottom using a small piece of cellophane tape that is about ½" (1 cm) square.

8. On the front, tape the thread so it meets the kite at the bridle point.

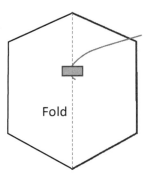

Fold

9. Crease the kite with a slight "V" shape. This will help it fly best. Check this "top view" before every flight:

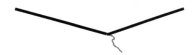

10. The kite will fly smoothly while you walk. Vary your pace to see what speed flies best.

Folded paper kite plan

Difficulty	Easy
Time to build:	20 minutes
Size:	8.5" x 11" (22 cm x 28 cm)

This folded paper kite is very inexpensive to build and the materials are easy to find. It's great for building kites on a budget. You can reuse scrap paper from junk mail, a telephone book, a paper booklet, or copy paper.

Materials:

- SAIL: Paper 8.5" x 11" (20 cm x 28 cm)
- SPARS: Coffee stirrer or drinking straw without a bend
- TAIL: 4' (122 cm) x 1" (2.5 cm) of marking tape or strips cut from a plastic bag
- LINE: Thread

Tools:

- Pen
- Ruler
- Paper punch
- Cellophane tape

Method:

1. Cut a page to size 8.5″ x 11″ (22 cm x 28 cm). This colorful piece of junk mail is a great choice:

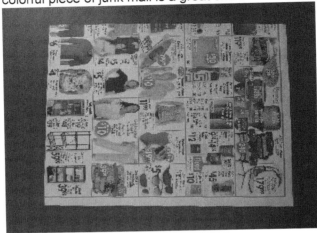

2. Fold the 11″ (28 cm) side of the paper in half. Make sure all edges are equal and straight.

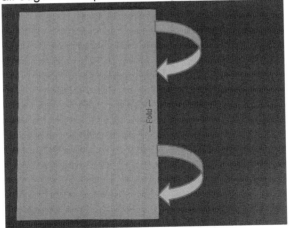

60

3. Take the bottom right <u>folded</u> edge and fold it to touch the left side. It should look like this before you crease it:

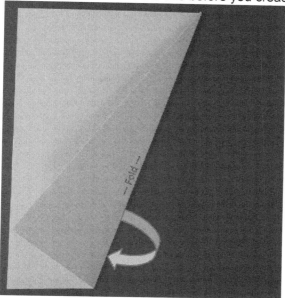

4. Take the top-left corner and open it to see the back.

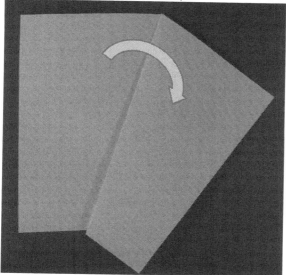

5. Tape the straw on one corner of the back. Wendy's has 9" (23 cm) straws that work perfectly. A wooden coffee stirrer works well once you cut it to 9" (23 cm). Notice that it should be a bit short of meeting the opposite corner:

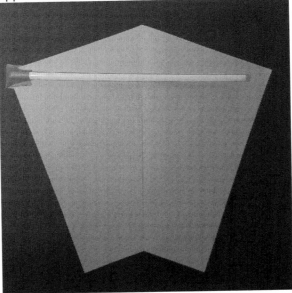

6. Tape the opposite corner and notice the gap between the straw and the paper. That creates a dihedral that helps it fly better.

7. Tape the 4' (122 cm) tail in the very center at the bottom.

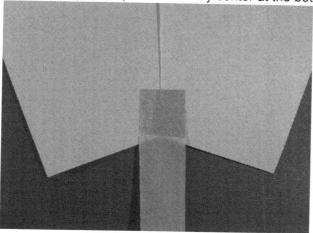

8. Turn the kite over to see the front. That's the side with the keel, not the side with the spar and tail.

9. Fold a piece of tape over the edge to prevent the string from tearing the paper.

10. Carefully measure 2.5" (6.3 cm) from the top of the kite and make a mark on the keel.

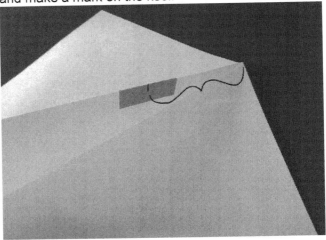

11. Use a paper punch to create a hole for your string. The size and shape of the hole is not important. Push the thread through the hole and tie a knot:

12. Make sure the keel is upright.

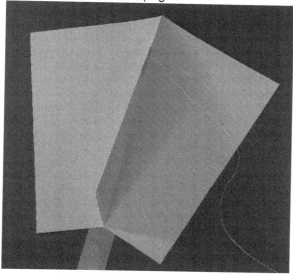

13. You're ready to fly!

Difficulty:	Easy
Time to build:	20 minutes
Size:	18" (45 cm) tall

Here's an easy kite to build that combines a paper clip with straws that you can find at any fast food restaurant!

Materials:
- SAIL: Tissue paper 18" x 18" (45 cm x 45 cm)
- SPARS: Four straws 9" (22.5 cm) long
  Important: The straws must not have an elbow.
- SPARS: Standard metal paper clip
- TAIL: A tall 13 gallon kitchen plastic bag
- LINE: Heavy duty thread

Tools:
- Scissors
- Cellophane tape
- Ruler
- Marker

Method:
1. Cut out the sail.

2. Fold in half.

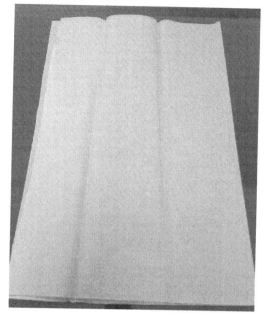

3. Mark 18" tall.

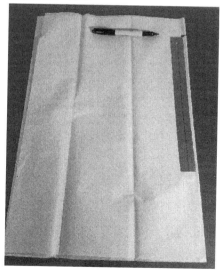

4. Measure 4" down from the top and draw a 9" horizontal line:

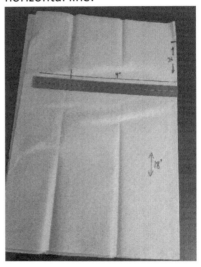

5. From that point, draw a line to the top and a line to the bottom:

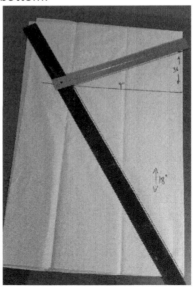

6. Unfold.

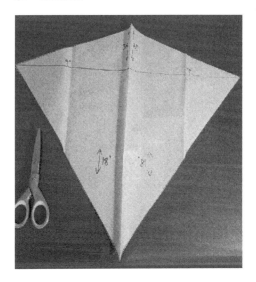

7. Take two straws and insert one straw into the other about ½ inch (1 cm) deep. Wrap the connection with 2 wraps of clear tape to give it strength. This is the vertical spine.

8. Tape the spine onto the tissue paper by folding tape over the top and bottom.

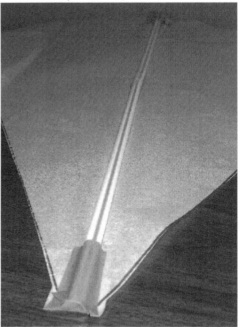

9. Straighten out the paper clip and bend this angle into it:

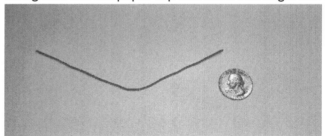

10. Tape the paper clip to the outside of the two straws, one on each side. This is the horizontal spreader.

11. Tape the spreader onto the tissue paper by first taping the center of the paper clip to the center of the horizontal line. Then tape the left and right corners.

12. Make a hole through the tissue and connect the flying line to the front at the center of the paper clip.

13. Tape on two tails to the bottom that are 4' (1.2 m) made from a plastic bag. (See the section called, "How to make tails from recycled plastic bags.")

14. Fly it gently in light wind or walk with it indoors. You can adjust the bend of the paper clip to suit the wind.

The comics newspaper delta kite plan

Difficulty:	Easy
Time to build:	40 minutes
Size:	13 ½" x 27" (34 cm x 69 cm)

This is a newspaper delta kite plan by Dennis L. Kucmerowski. It was published in in the spring 1988 issue of Kite Lines magazine.

Materials:

- SAIL: (2) Sheets of newspaper, one double-page and one single-page
- SPARS: The spars are made from rolled newspaper!
- TAIL: None
- LINE: Any kite line

Tools:

- Pen
- Ruler
- Scissors
- Paper punch
- Cellophane tape
- Dowel or rod 1/8" (0.32 cm) diameter x 24" long (60cm)

Method:

See the article called, "The Comics Kite, or The DK Delta" in the spring 1988 issue of Kite Lines magazine, page 36.

http://www.kitelife.com/wp-content/uploads/2012/01/Kite-Lines-v7-1.pdf

Plastic Kites

Hand drawn plastic fighter kite by Paul Berard.

Drinking straw Eddy kite plan

Difficulty:	Easy
Time to build:	20 minutes
Size:	8" x 8" (20 x 20 cm)

This kite is simple. It's made with two drinking straws and a plastic bag. You could use tissue paper instead of the plastic.

Materials:

- SAIL: (1) Plastic grocery bag
- SPARS: (2) Drinking straws
  Important: the straws must not have an elbow!
- TAIL: 1" (2.5 cm) strips from a grocery bag
- LINE: Thread

Tools:

- Scissors
- Marker
- Cellophane tape

Method:

1. Find a thin, plastic grocery bag.

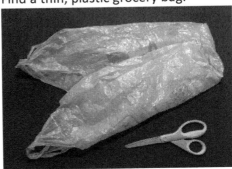

2. Cut off the handles, cut off the bottom, and cut along the side so that you have a long, flat sheet:

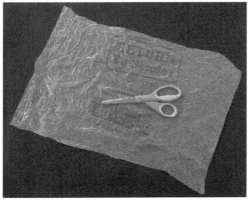

3. Fold the sheet in half.

4. Place one straw along the folded edge of the sheet. Note: If you'd like a certain part of the plastic bag to appear on the kite, move the straw up or down along the edge of the sheet until you include the design.

5. Mark the folded sheet at the top and bottom of straw.

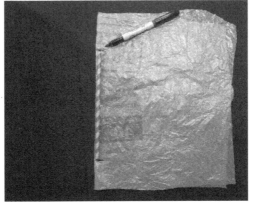

6. Place the second straw ¼ down from the top and half way across. Mark that location:

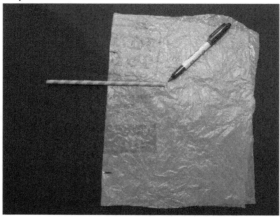

7. Use the straw as a straight edge to draw the outline connecting the three marks.

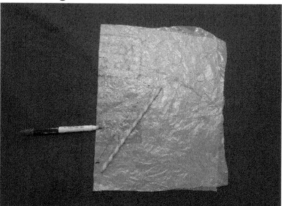

8. While folded, cut along the outline. This will cut both sides at the same time. By cutting both sides at once the kite will be exactly the same on the left and right sides. It's faster too.

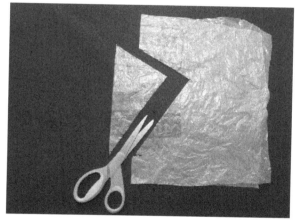

9. Open the sheet and lay it flat.

10. Decorate the front of the kite using markers.

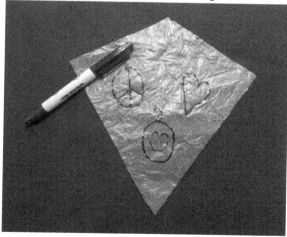

11. Tape the straws in place on the back of the kite using 1.5" (4 cm) piece of tape. Fold the tape over onto front.

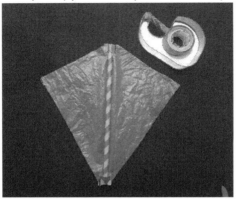

12. Cut second straw in half.

13. Place straw halves in the corners.

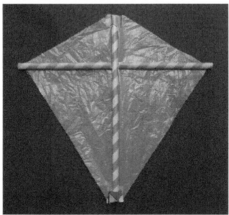

14. Tape them in place: left, and right.

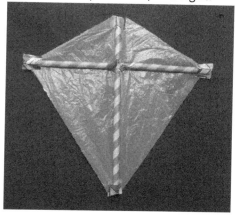

15. Bring the ends of the straws up and add a 2" (5 cm) piece of tape to the center to hold them in place:

16. Create a tail that's 1" (2.5cm) wide and seven (7) times the length of the straw. Use tape to attach sections of the tail into one long tail. See the section above called, "How to make tails from recycled plastic bags."

17. Tape the tail onto the back of the kite at the bottom:

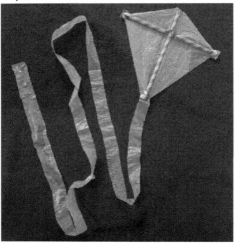

18. Turn your kite over to the front side. (The straws are on the back.)

19. Make two holes with the scissors as shown below.

20. Starting on the **front** of the kite, pass the thread through one hole, around the straws and back out the second hole to the front.

21. Tie a knot on the **front** of the kite:

22. Your kite is ready to fly!

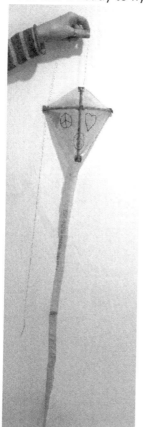

Difficulty:	Easy
Time to build:	20 minutes
Size:	24" x 18" (61 cm x 46 cm)

This is a simple kite to build that flies well in a variety of winds and can be decorated easily.

Materials:

- SAIL: Tyvek sheet or a tall 13 gallon (50 L) plastic kitchen garbage bag. Optionally, see "Joining sheets with tape"
- SPARS: (2) 16" (40 cm) x 1/8" (3 mm) wood dowels/bamboo
- TAILS: (2) 1" (2.5 cm) wide x 4' (122 cm) long using plastic scraps or flagging tape (tails are optional)
- LINE: Cotton string, heavy button thread, or yarn
- BRIDLE: 48" (122 cm) of your flying line

Tools:

- Ruler, Scissors
- Hole punch
- Tape: Strapping tape or clear cellophane tape
- Template: Cardboard or paper 18" (45 cm) x 24" (60 cm)

Paper sled kite built by Art St. Pierre.

Method:

1. Draw a grid on paper or cardboard with 6" (15 cm) for each square, so it's 18" (45 cm) tall x 12" (30 cm) wide:

2. Draw two diagonal lines to complete the outline of the template.

3. Cut along the dark lines. The half-template is complete.

Note: It's easy to build this kite using a 13 gallon (50 L) plastic garbage bag because the plastic is large enough and is already folded in half.

4. If you use a plastic grocery bag you will need to make a sheet of plastic that's 18" (45 cm) x 24" (60 cm) by cutting off the handles and cutting off the bottom seam.

5. Cut the bag open so that it is one flat sheet.

6. Fold the plastic sheet in half.

7. The plastic is folded in half with the folded edge on the right.

8. While the sheet is folded, cut out your sail along the outside line of the template.

9. Unfold. Optional: Decorate it with markers.

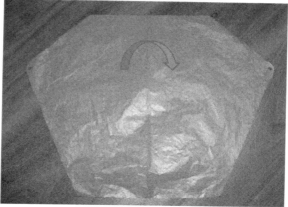

10. Reinforce the left and right corners with tape:

11. Punch two identical holes ½" (1.5 cm) from each corner. <u>Hint</u>: hold them together and punch both at the same time.

12. Cut two vertical spars from the 1/8" (3 mm) wooden dowels that are the same height as the kite.

13. Make sure the two spars are identical in length, then tape them to the back of the sail. The tape should be folded over at the top and the bottom. By folding the tape over you form a pocket for each spar.

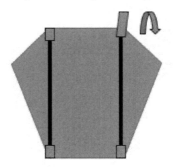

14. Cut a 48" (122 cm) piece of your flying line to use as the bridle

15. Tie each end to the punched holes in the sail:

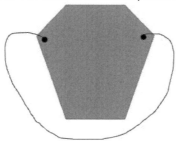

16. Hold the punched holes together to help find center of the bridle then tie a loop that is 2" (5 cm):

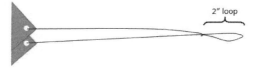

17. Attach the end of your flying line to the loop.

18. Optional: Create two tails of equal length that are 4' (122 cm) long and 1" (2.5 cm) wide. Tape them to the bottom corners:

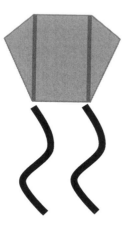

19. Decorate the front and fly your kite with the sticks on the back!

Plastic Bag Eddy kite plan

Difficulty:	Easy
Time to build:	60 minutes
Size:	24" (60 cm)

This is an Eddy kite made from a plastic bag. In this project you use a tension line to force the spreader into a bow.

Materials:
- SAIL: Plastic bag or garbage bag
- SPARS: Wood dowels (2) 24" (30 cm) long
- TAIL: Strips of the plastic bag
- LINE: String

Tools:
- Scissors
- Masking tape
- String
- Popsicle stick
- Ruler

Method:

http://spinsandneedles.com/stuff/2009/08/31/diy-kite-making-using-recycled-materials/

Note: To improve the flight of this kite, measure how tall the kite is, then place the spreader (that's the horizontal stick) ¼ of the way down from the very top of the kite.

Note: Some people feel the need to reinforce the edge of the sail using tape or string. This is not necessary.

250 feet (76 m) long train of 50 plastic bag kites by Paul Berard.

Dry Cleaner bag quad-line kite plan

Difficulty:	Easy
Time to build:	60 minutes
Size:	80" (200 cm) x 108" (274 cm)

This is a very unusual kite that flies like a jellyfish. It will fly indoors while you walk backwards and it will give you a slow, twisty introduction to flying a quad-line kite.

Materials:

- SAIL: (2) Dry Cleaner bags 20" (50 cm) x 54" (137 cm) – use the bags that are free and thin, not the heavy-duty storage bags
- SPARS: None
- TAIL: None
- LINE: Four pieces of thin polyester or Spectra line that are each 12' long
- HANDLES: (2) Chopsticks or (2) plastic clothes hangers

Tools:

- Scissors
- Ruler
- Hole punch
- Clear shipping tape
- Cellophane tape
- Masking tape

Method:

1. Lay one of the bags on the floor. Cut off the bottom, cut the side of the bag, and open it flat as one large sheet.

2. Do the same thing as step-1 to flatten the second bag.

3. Stretch the two bags out on the floor side-by-side. Hold them in place with masking tape to make it easier for the next step.

4. Tape the two bags together with shipping tape:

5. Reinforce the outline with cellophane tape:

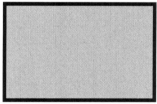

6. Reinforce each of the four corners with a 3" (5 cm) square of shipping tape.

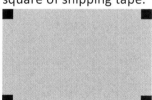

7. Measure four identical lines that are each 12' (350 cm).

8. Punch a hole in each of the four corner squares.

9. Attach one line to each of the four corner squares.
    Close-up view of one corner:

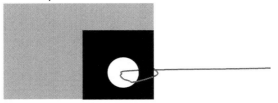

10. Wash the pair of chopsticks in soap and water. These
    will be the handles for your kite. If you'd like longer
    handles, use old plastic clothes hangers.

11. Make a notch ¼" (6 mm) from the top and bottom of
    each chopstick.

12. Attach the lines from the left side to one handle and
    then attach the lines from the right side to the other
    handle.

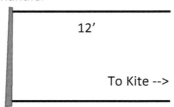

12'

To Kite -->

13. Fly the kite in a gymnasium

14. Have a friend help launch the kite while you walk backwards.

15. Quad-line flying is fun but it takes practice!

Plastic table cloth pointer kite plan

Difficulty:	Easy
Time to build:	60 minutes
Size:	11' (335 cm) long plus tail

This kite uses a plastic table cloth and organic materials that can be grown or found outdoors.

Materials:

- SAIL: Thin plastic sheet such as a plastic table cover, often re-purposed after an event.
- SPARS: Jerusalem artichoke stems
- TAIL: 6' (2 m) length of marking tape. This is also called "Surveyor's tape or "flagging tape." Another alternative is to tape together 1" (2.5 cm) wide strips until 6' (2m) long.
- LINE: One spool of kite string
- OTHER: Rubber bands, bamboo skewers, 2-liter soda bottle

Tools:

- Ruler
- Scissors
- Utility knife
- Strapping or shipping tape

Method:

See the post by EcoFlyer on instructables.com for plans: http://www.instructables.com/id/Building-a-low-cost-Pointer-kite/

Nylon Kites

This kite was built by Robert Reed Llewellyn using a 5x8 foot Welsh flag for the upper sail and lightweight ripstop nylon tent material for the lower sail.

Large, durable kites can be built from nylon. Nylon is the most popular fabric for kites that are built or sold in stores today.

Nylon fabric is available online and at kite shops in a variety of colors. To find a source, use the "Internet Resources" section below.

To build a nylon kite yourself, a wide variety of plans are available in the plans database: http://www.kiteplans.org/

Tip: You may be able to recycle fabric from hot air balloons, sailboats, and parachutes. While these may not be ideal, you might find huge quantities that are free!

Tip: Avoid stretchy and porous materials such as cotton and silk. Nylon is recommended for most projects.

Tip: Since these fabrics require sewing, you can find used sewing machines at garage sales, online, or you might borrow one for the duration of your project.

Tip: Practice sewing with scraps of the same fabric that you plan to use for your kite. Check both sides of the stitching. If the thread isn't straight you may need to adjust the tension on your machine.

Recycled umbrella kite plan

Difficulty:	Moderate
Time to build:	2-3 hours
Size:	48" (122 cm) diameter

An umbrella typically has eight points so you will need four straight spars to complete this project. A long tail and some strong line are also necessary.

This kite is built using a method that's similar to a hexagonal kite or "Three Stick Kite." This style is also called an "Island Kite."

Materials:

• SAIL: nylon fabric from a broken or recycled umbrella
• SPARS: (4) bamboo spars 48" (122 cm) long
• TAIL: bed sheets torn into 3" wide strips
• LINE: 50 to 100 lb. test kite line

Tools:

• Sewing machine

Method:

1. Take two bamboo spars and tie their centers together forming an "X" shape.

2. Take another two bamboo spars and tie their centers together to form a "+" shape:

3. Tie the two shapes together at the center to form a star:

4. Tie string around the ends of all the spars until they are held apart equally.

5. Cover the spars with the fabric from an umbrella and use tape to hold the fabric in place.

6. Sew pockets into each corner to hold the spars in place:

7. Attach a tail that's ten times the length of the kite.

8. Attach a three-point bridle at these locations. See the section called, "The Bridle."

9. Attach flying line to the bridle.

10. Fly the kite using 50 to 100 pound test line.

Example:

Here is the same kite built with three sticks. Notice the tape that holds the plastic and also notice the three point bridle:

Example:

Here is an example of the kite built with four sticks. There are hummers at the top and each color of tissue paper has string to reinforce its edges. This kite originates in Bermuda.

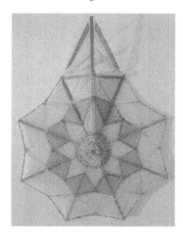

Free kite plans online

There is a huge database of kite plans for single, dual, quad, and miscellaneous kites. It is billed as "the world's largest kite plan archive." There are fighter kites, Japanese kites, bowed kites, rotor kites, airfoils, messengers, kite lights, and much more.

See: http://www.kiteplans.org/

Ghost kite built with Tyvek and dowels.

How to improvise your own kite

Size:	You choose
Difficulty:	Depends on your kite
Time to build:	Depends on your kite

You can build a kite of your own design. If you follow some basic steps you'll be amazed at what you can build and fly! This is a recipe for fun but you should understand that you are accepting the risk that sometimes your project will not fly. Keep in mind that kites are deceptively simple. Small changes in the symmetry, shape, tail, or bridle may be needed to change a kite that stays on the ground into a successful flying kite. Even after the kite is built you can still experiment and make changes!

Improvising a kite is often treated as an **art project** when in reality it is an **engineering project**. For that reason you may need an expert on hand to rework a design into a kite that is capable of flight.

Example:

The original painting and design concept may need to be reworked to be symmetric, with balance and flexibility. A two-point, three-point, or four-point bridle may be necessary to support the kite. The framework may need to be strengthened or reduced in weight. Tension lines may help some kites and long tails may not be desired but it may be necessary to enable certain constructions to fly.

Materials:

To improvise a kite, start by collecting the materials for your kite. These include a variety of recycled items, such as:

- Sails: paper, plastic, trash bags, wrappers, foam trays, paper cups, junk mail
- String: heavy duty button thread, yarn
- Spars: bamboo, food skewers, old blinds, wood sticks, straws
- Tails: streamers, ribbon, strips of plastic

Requirements:

Use your artistic creativity as much as possible and use your imagination to make your kite creative and unique. This could be a variation on a standard design or add decorations that give your kite character.

Here are a few suggestions that will give your kite a strong chance for success:

- Include long, colorful tails that are seven times the length of the kite. Attach them to the bottom at the center.
- Use a vertical spine in the exact center.
- Use a symmetric design. Fold the sail in half, then cut out the sail with scissors or razor so the left side is exactly identical to the right.
- Use lightweight, recycled materials.
- Consider building a *variation* of an Eddy or Sled kite from the plans in this book. Both are great fliers.
- When given the opportunity to improvise a kite, many people build a flat kite. Instead, consider including a curved bow shape in the design instead of a flat form.

Construct your kite:

While your kite should be creative and unique, your primary goal is to make the kite fly.

These kites look great, but they're unbridled.

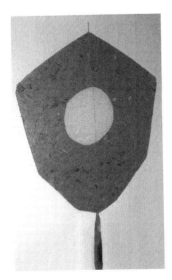 

The bridle is not a finishing touch. It is one of the most essential features of making a kite fly. Carefully read the earlier sections above about how to balance and bridle your kite.

Tip: Repeat this motto: "Bridle on the front, spars on the back, tail at the bottom."

Supplies

Line

Search Amazon or eBay for "kite string," "kite handle," or "kite winder."
AKA kite store offers kite string on handles for 34 cents: http://kite.org/kitetalk/index.php?/store/product/202-plastic-kite-handle-w-line/
Drachen Foundation offers plastic winders: http://drachenstore.easystorecreator.net/items/kite-kits/materials-/kite-string-with-plastic-winder-e010-detail.htm
Available from Gayla Industries in Houston, TX http://www.gaylainc.com/site/kites/
Check your local craft stores or balloon suppliers.
Button thread is a heavy-duty thread that can be found in sewing stores.
Baker's twine is available from many supermarkets.
In a pinch you can use dental floss but it's more expensive than kite string on a winder. The strength of dental floss is 10# to 15#.

Spars

Bamboo food skewers are available at supermarkets.
Craft stores sell a bamboo package with 40 pieces that are 12" (30 cm) long for about $2.50.
1/8" (3mm) wooden dowels can be purchased from many crafts stores and hardware stores. They are usually color coded "red."

Pier 1 Imports sells matchstick bamboo window blinds. Sometimes you can buy the leftover/broken ones at a discount.
Bamboo is available from http://drachenstore.easystorecreator.net/items/kite-kits/materials-/Bamboo-detail.htm
Cindoco Wood Products Co. in Ohio is www.cindoco.com
SchoolSpecialty.com has 36" (90 cm) x 1/8" (3 mm) wooden dowels in 10 packs.
You can buy dowels in bulk from 1-800-242-9663. There is a $50 minimum.
You can buy wooden dowels from S&S Wood Specialty in Westbrook, Maine.

Sails

Trash bags are available at supermarkets and hardware stores.
Trash bags are available from Bear Packaging & Supply Inc in Mt. Pleasant, MI.
Ripstop nylon is available from many online kite vendors.
Tyvek is available on the "materials" page http://drachenstore.easystorecreator.net/

Tails

Make your own tails as described in the section called, "How to make tails from recycled plastic bags."

Hardware stores carry rolls of "marking tape." It is also called, "flagging tape" or "surveyor's tape." It is perfect for tails because it does not have any adhesive.

Crepe paper is available from party supply stores but it tears very easily.

Tape

Clear plastic tape or Scotch tape are available at all stationary and crafts stores.

"Strapping Tape" is much stronger than plastic tape but it is slightly heavier. It is available from Staples and Walmart.

Address labels are a possible substitute for tape because they're already cut to size.

Kite Plans

Kite Plans Database http://www.kiteplans.org/

Drachen Foundation kite plans and materials
http://www.drachen.org/learn/drachen-kite-plans-materials

Simple kites http://www.instructables.com/howto/kite/

Kites in the Classroom free book with plans
http://classroom.KitingUSA.com

Contest ideas

Collect a pile of materials and challenge others to build kites from materials you've gathered. See the section above describing, "How to improvise your own kite."

Give prizes for:

- Steadiest flyer
- Highest
- Most artistic and beautiful
- Best use of materials
- Most innovative use of recycled materials
- Smallest and largest kites (they must fly!)

After the contest, create an online photo exhibit of your recycled kites.

"When I was young I made a five foot tall kite from three sticks of bamboo and covered it with newspaper and made the tails made from bedsheets. I put razor blades on the outside edges, on the rope, and at the bottom of the tail so I could fight with other kites"

- Dr. Raul E. Velez

Feedback and suggestions

Do you have a favorite technique, kite plan, or kite material to share? Send email with ideas and suggestions to: davisong@verizon.net

A paper Japanese Sode kite with a brush painted design.

Made in the USA
Columbia, SC
26 February 2022

56591367R00061